This Journal Belongs To:

_____

The most exhausting thing you can be is N.O.T. yourself!

Fresh Manna

Shawanda R. Randolph

JUST BECAUSE EVERYONE WANTS TO BE A PART OF YOUR CIRCLE DOES NOT MEAN THEY CAN HANDLE THE WEIGHT OF WHAT IS IN YOUR CIRCLE. UNDERSTAND THE INTRICACIES OF YOUR TEAM.

Fresh Manna
Shawanda R. Randolph

JUST BECAUSE EVERYONE WANTS TO BE A PART OF YOUR CIRCLE DOES NOT MEAN THEY CAN HANDLE THE WEIGHT OF WHAT IS IN YOUR CIRCLE. UNDERSTAND THE INTRICACIES OF YOUR TEAM

Fresh Manna
Shawanda R. Randolph

JUST BECAUSE EVERYONE WANTS TO BE
A PART OF YOUR CIRCLE DOES NOT
MEAN THEY CAN HANDLE THE WEIGHT
OF WHAT IS IN YOUR CIRCLE
UNDERSTAND THE INTRICACIES OF
YOUR TEAM

Fresh Manna
Shawanda R. Randolph

JUST BECAUSE EVERYONE WANTS TO BE A PART OF YOUR CIRCLE DOES NOT MEAN THEY CAN HANDLE THE WEIGHT OF WHAT IS IN YOUR CIRCLE. UNDERSTAND THE INTRICACIES OF YOUR TEAM.

JUST BECAUSE EVERYONE WANTS TO BE A PART OF YOUR CIRCLE DOES NOT MEAN THEY CAN HANDLE THE WEIGHT OF WHAT IS IN YOUR CIRCLE. UNDERSTAND THE INTRICACIES OF YOUR TEAM.

Fresh Manna
Shawanda R. Randolph

JUST BECAUSE EVERYONE WANTS TO BE A PART OF YOUR CIRCLE DOES NOT MEAN THEY CAN HANDLE THE WEIGHT OF WHAT IS IN YOUR CIRCLE. UNDERSTAND THE INTRICACIES OF YOUR TEAM.

Fresh Manna
Shawanda R. Randolph

JUST BECAUSE EVERYONE WANTS TO BE A PART OF YOUR CIRCLE DOES NOT MEAN THEY CAN HANDLE THE WEIGHT OF WHAT IS IN YOUR CIRCLE. UNDERSTAND THE INTRICACIES OF YOUR TEAM.

Fresh Manna
Shawanda R. Randolph

JUST BECAUSE EVERYONE WANTS TO BE
A PART OF YOUR CIRCLE DOES NOT
MEAN THEY CAN HANDLE THE WEIGHT
OF WHAT IS IN YOUR CIRCLE.
UNDERSTAND THE INTRICACIES OF
YOUR TEAM.

Fresh Manna
Shawanda R. Randolph

JUST BECAUSE EVERYONE WANTS TO BE A PART OF YOUR CIRCLE DOES NOT MEAN THEY CAN HANDLE THE WEIGHT OF WHAT IS IN YOUR CIRCLE. UNDERSTAND THE INTRICACIES OF YOUR TEAM.

Fresh Manna
Shawonda R. Randolph

JUST BECAUSE EVERYONE WANTS TO BE A PART OF YOUR CIRCLE DOES NOT MEAN THEY CAN HANDLE THE WEIGHT OF WHAT IS IN YOUR CIRCLE. UNDERSTAND THE INTRICACIES OF YOUR TEAM.

Fresh Manna
Showonda R. Randolph

JUST BECAUSE EVERYONE WANTS TO BE A PART OF YOUR CIRCLE DOES NOT MEAN THEY CAN HANDLE THE WEIGHT OF WHAT IS IN YOUR CIRCLE. UNDERSTAND THE INTRICACIES OF YOUR TEAM.

JUST BECAUSE EVERYONE WANTS TO BE A PART OF YOUR CIRCLE DOES NOT MEAN THEY CAN HANDLE THE WEIGHT OF WHAT IS IN YOUR CIRCLE. UNDERSTAND THE IMPORTANCE OF YOUR TEAM

Fresh Manna
Shawanda R. Randolph

JUST BECAUSE EVERYONE WANTS TO BE A PART OF YOUR CIRCLE DOES NOT MEAN THEY CAN HANDLE THE WEIGHT OF WHAT IS IN YOUR CIRCLE. UNDERSTAND THE INTRICACIES OF YOUR TEAM.

NEVER DOWN PLAY YOUR GIFTS, TALENTS OR SKILLS TO FIT IN!

Fresh Manna
Shavonda R. Randolph

JUST BECAUSE EVERYONE WANTS TO BE A PART OF YOUR CIRCLE DOES NOT MEAN THEY CAN HANDLE THE WEIGHT OF WHAT IS IN YOUR CIRCLE. UNDERSTAND THE INTRICACIES OF YOUR TEAM.

Fresh Manna
Showanda R. Randolph

www.ingramcontent.com/pod-product-compliance
Lightning Source LLC
Chambersburg PA
CBHW071251070526
44583CB00017B/2425